Markievicz
The Rebel Countess

Aristocrat, artist and revolutionary, Constance Markievicz became involved in the struggle for Irish independence and was sentenced to death for her part in the 1916 Rising. Her sentence was later commuted to penal servitude and she went on to become the first woman government minister in Europe.

Media Reaction to the Series
'Short, entertaining and full of great pictures'
The Irish Times

'This is a very good idea – a series of easy to read biographies of major figures, past and present'
Ireland of the Welcomes

'Easily digestible for young impatient readers'
Sunday Tribune

THE AUTHORS

MARY MORIARTY
Lives in Dublin with her husband and three children. She took a degree with the Open University in arts and has taught in the Adult Literacy scheme in Dun Laoghaire.

CATHERINE SWEENEY
Took a degree in arts at U.C.D. Has worked as a teacher at secondary level and as a translator. She lives in Dublin with her husband and children.

Books in this series

No.1 Wolfe Tone
Tone, the most famous of the United Irishmen, secured French aid to help bring democracy and freedom to Ireland.

No.2 W.B. Yeats
Ireland's best-loved poet, winner of the Nobel Prize for literature.

No.3 Granuaile
Chieftain and pirate, the terror of the western seas during the reign of Elizabeth I.

No. 4 Bob Geldof
Rock musician who united the world for a day in the cause of famine-starved Ethiopia.

No.5 Jonathan Swift
Writer, satirist and beloved dean of St. Patrick's Cathedral, Dublin.

No. 6 Markievicz
The 'Rebel Countess' who believed in Irish nationalism and fought in 1916. Strong supporter of women's rights, and first woman elected to the Westminster parliament.

O'Brien Junior Biography Library No.6

MARKIEVICZ

The Rebel Countess

MARY MORIARTY
&
CATHERINE SWEENEY

Drawings by
DONALD TESKEY

THE O'BRIEN PRESS
DUBLIN

First published 1991 by The O'Brien Press Ltd.,
20 Victoria Road, Dublin 6, Ireland.

10 9 8 7 6 5 4 3 2 1

British Library Cataloguing in Publication Data
Moriarty, Mary
Countess Markievicz (O'Brien junior biography library
ISSN 0790-9675;v.6)
1.Ireland. Markievicz, Constance Georgina
I.Title II.Sweeney, Catherine
941.5081092
ISBN 0-86278-211-2

Typesetting: The O'Brien Press
Cover design: The Graphiconies, Dublin
Cover separations: The City Office, Dublin
Printing: Colour Books Ltd., Dublin

Contents

Childhood 7

The Land League 11

Life at the Big House 13

High Society in London and Dublin 14

Art School 18

Paris 20

Casimir Markievicz 22

A London Wedding 23

Return to Dublin 25

Involvement in Nationalism 27

Political Life 30

The Fianna 33

Poverty in Dublin 38

The 1913 Lock Out 41

The Home Rule Struggle 45

O'Donovan-Rossa's Funeral 46

Planning a Rebellion 50

Persuading MacNeill 52

The Easter Rising 53

Death Sentence and the Executions 57

Prison 58 and 60

Free Again 61

The Rise of Sinn Féin 63

Minister for Labour 65

The Truce and the Treaty 69

Civil War 71

Final Campaign 73

Bibliography 76

Places to Go and Things to See 77

Events of the Day 78

Lissadell House in Sligo where Constance grew up, still stands today.

In 1868 in London a young couple, Henry and Georgina Gore-Booth, were anxiously awaiting the birth of their first child. Georgina was English, from Tickhill Castle in York-shire and Henry was Irish, the son of Sir Robert and Lady Gore-Booth of Sligo. They were staying in Henry's family townhouse in London – a large mansion near Buckingham Palace. On 4 February their baby was born, a girl they called Constance. She was to grow up to be beautiful, talented and courageous. Many years later, under her married name, Countess Markievicz, she became known and loved throughout Ireland for her kindness to the poor, for the brave part she played in the 1916 Rising and as the first woman ever to be elected to the British Parliament.

Shortly after her birth Constance was brought back to Ireland by her parents. After a long journey they finally reached their home in Sligo, a magnificent stately home called Lissadell. This house had been built thirty years earlier by Henry's father, Sir Robert. The young couple were glad to be back in their beautiful home surrounded by trees, with parklands that ran down to the sea and the sands. The house, which is still standing, has forty-eight rooms and a driveway four kilometres long. Here Con-stance spent her childhood, as she describes it, 'On a beautiful, enchanted Western coast where we grew up intimate with the soft mists and the coloured mountains and where each morning, you woke to the sound of the wild birds.'

The Gore-Booth family were wealthy landlords. They owned thousands of acres of land around Sligo which they rented to more than a thousand tenant farmers. The income this brought in made them one of the richest families in Sligo.

They belonged to a class of people known as the Anglo-Irish. At the time of Constance's childhood – the 1870s – the Gore-Booth family was well established in Sligo. The first member of their family to come to Ireland was an

Englishman, Captain Paul Gore, who arrived in 1598 with Elizabeth I's army. This army came to put down the rebellion against English rule led by Hugh O'Neill and Hugh Roe O'Donnell. Captain Gore was a successful soldier and as a reward for his services he was granted lands in Sligo; lands which had been taken from the native Irish as punishment for their part in the rebellion. Over the next hundred years or so the family's land-holdings increased as a result of wars and the laws that were passed preventing the native Irish from owning land.

During the 1870s, Ireland was part of the British Empire ruled by the British Government from London and most of Ireland was owned by Anglo-Irish landlords. There was usually a great divide between the Anglo-Irish landlords and their tenants. The landlords had a different religion, culture and language. As Lady Fingall, one of the Anglo-Irish landlord class of the time, said: 'The Irish landlords lived within their demesnes making a world of their own with Ireland outside the gates.'

Constance had a very happy childhood at Lissadell. The big house was always full of friends, relations and servants and there was always plenty of activity. She had brothers and sisters to play with too. Her brother Josselyn was born when she was a year old and her sister, Eva, a year later. Another sister, Mabel, was born four years later in 1874 and her youngest brother Mordaunt in 1876 when Constance was eight. But her special friend in the family was her sister Eva. Whereas Constance was headstrong and noisy, Eva was quiet and thoughtful. Despite this the two sisters had a very close and loving relationship which lasted throughout their lives.

Constance was a happy, outgoing child, always on the go and full of mischief. At an early age her father taught her to ride and shoot. By the time she was six she had her own pony, Storeen, though she was only allowed to trot Storeen up and down the driveway led by one of the servants. This annoyed Constance and one day she kicked her pony into a gallop and flew off over the fields leaving

Constance gallops off on her pony, Storeen.

the poor astonished servant far behind. She eventually came back, after a long gallop over the countryside having proved she was well able to handle Storeen on her own. From then on she was allowed to go riding wherever she liked.

She loved the freedom and excitement of riding through the fields and lanes around Lissadell and became a well-known figure in the area. The family butler described her as 'everything that was nice and good, always full of life and energy, and as innocent as the wild birds of the air; there was no guile in her, ever sympathetic, ever fond of an innocent joke.'

At about the same time she began her schooling. In those days the daughters of well-to-do families did not go to school but were taught at home by a governess. The governesses who came to teach at Lissadell must have had a hard time with Constance. She only paid attention to the subjects that interested her – literature and painting. She often skipped both meals and lessons and took off on Storeen around the countryside instead. She would be punished for these escapades when she came home by being sent to bed without her supper.

Constance was full of fun and laughter but she was also very kind. Sometimes when herself and Eva were out walking they would give their shoes or coats to some poor person they met. Constance would often call into the cottages of the country people, her father's tenants, bringing presents of food and other things. Most of these people were desperately poor. Their cabins consisted of just one room which housed the whole family as well as the donkey and cow. Usually their only furniture was a table and a couple of benches with straw for bedding, and they survived on a diet of milk, potatoes and oatmeal.

In spite of the poverty of his tenants Constance's father was considered a good landlord. He charged lower rents than many other landlords. He also spent most of his time on his estates and therefore was aware of the difficulties his tenants suffered. He would often reduce or forego the rent when someone was genuinely unable to pay. Many other landlords lived permanently in England and were either unaware of or indifferent to the distress of their tenants and as a result many tenants were evicted when they were unable to pay the rent.

The year of 1879, when Constance was eleven, was a year of exceptionally bad weather with very heavy rains. The potatoes and other crops failed. Throughout Ireland tenant farmers faced ruin and starvation. Many of the older people remembered the disastrous famine of the 1840s when more than one million people died of hunger and there was widespread fear that the same thing was going to happen again.

Fortunately the crop failure of 1879 wasn't as serious as the Great Famine. Nevertheless, as all tenants depended on their crops for an income, many were unable to pay their rent. During 1879 and 1880 over 16,000 families were evicted from their homes for not paying rent.

The Lissadell tenants were luckier. Sir Henry allowed them to pay whatever they could afford. The family brought in a large store of food and Constance and her brothers and sisters worked hard with their mother distributing this food to the starving tenants who queued at the kitchen door from early morning until night.

THE LAND LEAGUE

At this time in Ireland tenant farmers were living in poverty and misery. They could be thrown out of their homes by landlords even when they had paid their rent. There was no control on rents – the landlords could increase them anytime to whatever amount they wished. If tenants improved their house or land the landlord usually raised their rent because the value of the property had increased.

A man called Michael Davitt saw this misery and injustice and decided to do something about it. His own family had been evicted from their home when he was a small boy and had had to emigrate to England. In 1879 he set up an organisation called the Land League to help tenant

A family evicted from their home.

farmers. Charles Stewart Parnell, the leading Irish politician of the time, became President of the Land League and tenants flocked to join. For the first time they were being given a chance to stand up to the landlords. The League demanded that the Government should pass laws preventing the landlords from charging excessive rents or from evicting their tenants without just cause.

LIFE AT THE BIG HOUSE

While all this agitation was going on life continued as usual at Lissadell. The family, though aware of the Land League, was not particularly troubled by it; politics and Irish history were never discussed in the Gore-Booth home.

In summertime there were picnics on the beach, excursions on horseback through the countryside, fishing trips and games of cricket on the cricket lawn in front to the house. In winter there were hunting and shooting. In the evenings the family and other guests often staged plays in the drawingroom. They sometimes put these plays on in Sligo town to raise money for local charities. There were always guests staying in the house and the family would regularly go for long visits to other big houses. Constance had her own small boat and spent many happy hours sailing in the bay below the house. She was also a talented artist and spent a lot of time painting and drawing.

When she was fourteen she joined the Sligo Hunt and for the next ten years or so she went riding with the hunt every Tuesday and Friday during the winter. She quickly became known throughout Sligo for her courage and skill. The country people would exclaim as they saw the hunt go by, 'My God, Look at little Miss Gore. Isn't she great!'

The young poet William Butler Yeats, who stayed with his relations in Sligo for long periods and would later come to know Constance well, frequently saw her out riding. 'She had often passed me on horseback going or coming from the hunt and was the acknowledged beauty of the country. I heard now and then of some tomboyish feat or of her reckless riding but the general impression was that she was respected and admired.'

Yeats later wrote a poem describing Constance at this time:

When long ago I saw her ride
Under Ben Bulben to the meet,
The beauty of her country-side
With all youth's lonely wildness stirred,
She seemed to have grown clean and sweet
Like any rock-bred, sea-borne bird:

One of Constance's favourite sources of amusement was playing practical jokes. Sometimes these were just for fun, other times they were intended to teach people a lesson. Once, for example, two young men staying in the house were unkind to some poor people in the area. Constance dressed up as a beggar woman and approached them on the road, asking for money. The young men didn't recognise her and were very rude to her. They must have been very embarrassed when she revealed her identity.

HIGH SOCIETY IN LONDON AND DUBLIN

In 1887, when Constance was nineteen, she went to London to be presented at the court of Queen Victoria and to take part in the London Season. All the young daughters of the aristocracy were presented to the Queen when they reached this age. It was a ceremony that marked their entrance into adult society. Constance was presented on 17 March, looking very beautiful in a dress of white satin with a train that was nearly three metres long. Once the young debutantes had appeared at Court, they were swept up in the whirl of the London Season. This lasted from April to July and was a time of great gaiety and style, when wealthy British aristocrats held dances, parties and balls in their grand homes so that their sons and daughters could meet each other and, they hoped, find suitable marriage partners.

*Constance stops a fight on the streets
of London.*

Constance's friend, Lady Fingall, recalls how 'All the houses had bright newly watered window boxes. There were flowers everywhere and sunshine and jingling hansoms. It was great fun to be alive and young. There were Sunday parades in the park, where people walked up and down after church, met their friends and talked to them. The women were beautifully dressed. It was the time of big hats and full rustling silk dresses.'

Constance made a great impression on London society during her first season. Lady Fingall tells us she was 'much loved and admired'. She was 'a wild beautiful girl and all the young men wanted to dance with her. She was lovely and gay and she was the life and soul of any party.'

Although Constance threw herself into the spirit of the season with vigour, she was not blind to the plight of the less fortunate. One evening when she was coming home late from a party she saw a group of beggars sleeping on street benches. She ordered the carriage to stop, got out and divided all the money in her purse between the beggars. On another occasion she was driving in her carriage when she saw two drunk men fighting in the street. Afraid that they would get hurt she jumped down from the carriage and courageously put herself between them to stop the fight.

When the London Season ended the Gore-Booth family returned to Dublin to attend the Horse Show. The Dublin Horse Show was an important occasion for horse-loving landowners like the Gore-Booths. It was also a time when lavish parties were held in the elegant Georgian houses of the Irish aristocracy.

Dublin had a social season too, though it was shorter than the London Season, lasting just one month from mid-February to mid-March. The formal balls of the Dublin Season took place at Dublin Castle where the Viceroy held court. The Viceroy, sometimes called the Lord Lieutenant, was the British monarch's representative and the head of the British administration in Ireland. In 1888 Constance took part in her first Dublin Season. She stayed in Harcourt Terrace, in a house belonging to her cousins. Once again her great beauty and gaiety made her the centre of attraction at many of the parties.

For the next four years Constance took part in the London Season, the Horse Show and the Dublin Season. In between this social whirl she carried on with her usual activities: sailing, hunting, painting, visiting her friends in Ireland and England and receiving guests at Lissadell. One guest who visited Lissadell at this time was Mary Leslie from Castle Leslie in Co. Monaghan. Constance was out riding when she arrived so Mary went down to the shore to meet her 'I thought I had never seen anyone so lovely,' she later said, 'she started off at a hard gallop over the shore as if she feared the tide would come up and stop her. Hatless, dressed in a brown corduroy frock, not a habit, she was startlingly beautiful as the sun caught her fair hair.'

As time passed, however, the endless round of entertainments and social activities began to seem empty to Constance. She felt she needed some purpose in her life. In 1892 when she was in London once again for the season she skipped many of the parties and receptions and went to private art lessons instead. She was a talented artist and made rapid progress. She decided that what she wanted most of all was to become a full-time art student so she could devote herself entirely to art. However her family refused to give her permission.

They wanted her to find a suitable husband, get married and settle down like other women of her age. Much to their disappointment she had rejected all her suitors. It was a difficult time for Constance who was now twenty-five years old. We can judge her frustration from this note in her diary: 'If I could only cut the family tie and have a life and interest of my own I should want no other heaven.' She believed that life as an artist would give her freedom and independence and continued to beg her parents to allow her to study at art school.

Finally they gave in to her pleadings and in 1893 Constance enrolled at the Slade School of Art in London. She did not intend her art to be just a fashionable pastime. She hoped to earn her living as an artist so she worked very hard at the Slade and kept up her private lessons in the Bolton Studios. A fellow artist described the first time she saw Constance at the Boltons. 'The studios were full of artists in more or less shabby blouses, gay, hopeful and chattering. One day into their midst sailed Constance Gore-Booth in some long frock of the period which I can only remember as part of an enchanting picture.'

During the school holidays Constance returned home to Lissadell. Her parents were very hospitable and loved to have their children and their friends to stay. While in London, Constance had met Yeats, who was then making a name for himself as a poet and dramatist, and he was invited to join the family at Lissadell during the winter of 1894-5. Yeats found the Gore-Booths kind and well educated, 'Ever ready to take up new ideas and new things'. He introduced them to Irish folklore and poetry and told them of the great Gaelic revival that had started among his literary friends in Dublin. Years later he recalled his stay with them in the famous lines:

> The light of evening, Lissadell
> Great windows open to the south
> Two girls in silk kimonos, both
> Beautiful, one a gazelle.

While Constance continued her studies at the Slade, Eva, who the doctors suspected was suffering from the then deadly disease of consumption, was sent away to Italy in the hope that a milder, warmer climate would help her condition. Fortunately for Eva her family could afford to keep her in Italy for nearly a year and her health gradually improved. While convalescing she met an English woman,

Esther Roper, who was to change the course of her life. Esther Roper spent her life working for women's rights in the factories and slums of Manchester in the North of England. Eva was inspired by Esther's dedication and decided, much to her family's dismay, that when she was well enough she would join her.

On her return from Italy Eva told Constance and their youngest sister Mabel all about the suffrage movement. The movement had been set up in England to fight for women's rights including the right to vote. The three sisters set up a local committee to launch the movement in Sligo. A few weeks later, around Christmas time, they held a large meeting in Drumcliff schoolhouse which Constance, as President, chaired. Two-thirds of those present were men who had gone along to poke fun at the women. When Constance stood up to open the meeting there was much good-natured cheering and uproarious laughter. She took the banter well and later learned that the cause of all the fun was a huge bunch of mistletoe hanging from a rafter just above her head! This time the practical joke was on her. At the meeting she made her first public speech on a political issue and it was reported in the local press.

After Christmas Constance stayed on at Lissadell for the hunting season and in February the Gore-Booth girls attended a big fancy dress ball in Sligo, dressed as dairy-maids. This was partly a joke at their brother's expense. Josselyn had opened the Drumcliff Dairy Society the year before. This was the first co-operative creamery in Sligo and an enlightened action for a landlord in those days.

It was to be Eva's last ball. Soon afterwards she turned her back on high society and left Lissadell to spend the rest of her life living and working in the slums of Manchester and London. For the next thirty years she and Esther Roper campaigned for the rights of barmaids, pit girls, flower sellers, circus performers, factory hands and many others whom they felt were open to abuse or unjustly treated by society.

Constance too was about to take a step which would change her life. She decided to leave London and continue her art studies in Paris. In the late 1890s Paris was a very exciting place for an art student. It was the era of the Impressionist painters and Pierre Auguste Renoir, Edgar Degas and Claud Monet were among the famous painters working there.

Constance was accepted at Julian's art school. Though she had to work very hard, starting classes at eight o'clock every morning, she loved what she was doing. A fellow artist said of the school, it is a place where 'all distinctions disappear; you have neither name nor family ... you are yourself. You are an individual with art before you – art and nothing else.'

This environment suited Constance perfectly. She wore a ring on her wedding finger to show that she was married to art. She visited art exhibitions, saw and studied the art treasures at the famous Louvre Gallery, or sat for hours in the pavement cafés discussing art with her fellow students. They nicknamed her 'Velo' (French for 'bicycle') because she cycled everywhere. Though she was now thirty years old, she was still a tomboy. When another student teased her about her accent Constance dragged her to the nearest tap and held her head under it to teach her a lesson. She avoided the English students because they tended to stick together and when the Boer War, between the British and the Boers in South Africa, broke out she took an anti-British stance declaring, 'Je suis Irlandaise'.

Constance lived very modestly in a room on the Left Bank. She had a small allowance and when money was short she sometimes went hungry. But when funds were good, according to a friend, she was 'hopelessly generous'. She loved the Bohemian atmosphere of the student quarter and went to lots of parties and dances. It was at one of these that she met and fell in love with a Polish nobleman.

Constance and her sister, Eva, dressed as dairymaids.

Count Casimir Dunin Markievicz was a Polish aristocrat whose family had large estates in the Ukraine. He was a very tall handsome man with an attractive personality. When they met he had been studying art in Paris for about five years. Although he was six years younger than Constance he was a widower with a young son, Stanislas, who lived with his grandparents in the Ukraine.

A Polish writer who was with Casimir at the ball introduced them. Later he described Constance that night as being 'about twenty years of age and conspicuous by her proud bearing ... Her profile was delicately drawn and her eyes grey-blue.' Constance found Casimir romantic, exotic and fun to be with – very different from the staid English suitors she met during her London seasons. A few days after the ball, when the writer was sitting in a café, Casimir and Constance rode up on bicycles, laughing, chatting and teasing one another and obviously the best of friends.

From then on they went everywhere together. They both loved cycling which was all the rage. They often rode out to the Bois de Boulogne on the outskirts of Paris to picnic for the day. Casimir even entered the Paris-St. Malo bicycle race and near the finish was leading when his chain broke. Constance went to St. Malo to cheer him home.

He was also a champion fencer and when a Frenchman insulted Constance at a masked ball Casimir challenged him to a duel. She was dazzled by him. Later when Casimir settled in Dublin he founded a fencing club where he passed on his skill to the young men who joined.

Like Constance, Casimir had only a small allowance and when he was short of money he washed trams at night. In spite of being hard up they enjoyed themselves in Paris and by the end of the year 1899, they were engaged. To celebrate the event Casimir painted a large portrait of Constance. The painting called 'Constance in White' was shown at the Great Exhibition of Paris in 1900.

This was a very happy time for Constance. She wrote to tell Eva of her engagement, saying, 'I don't quite know when we shall be married but I wish it to be soon.' Sadly, her happiness was marred by the death of her beloved father. Sir Henry died in Switzerland in January 1900 and Con returned home to Lissadell to comfort her mother.

In May Casimir visited Lissadell to meet the Gore-Booth family before going home to the Ukraine for the summer. While he was away Lady Gore-Booth and Constance made arrangements for a September wedding in London. When Casimir arrived for the wedding Constance suddenly realised that he spoke very little English, so she taught him the marriage responses as they travelled around the city on the top deck of a bus – much to the amusement of their fellow passengers!

They were married on the 29 September 1900, three times, once in the Russian Legation, once in a registry office and finally in St. Mary's Church, Marylebone. They had a splendid though small wedding as the Gore-Booths were still in official mourning for Sir Henry.

Constance looked beautiful in a white satin dress trimmed with orange blossoms. Around her neck she wore sparkling diamonds and pearls, while Casimir was dashing in a Russian court uniform. Two of her four bridesmaids wore green to mark the Irish connection. After the reception the couple were seen off on the boat train from Victoria Station for their honeymoon in France. Having waved goodbye to the family Casimir and Constance jumped off the train at the next station and returned secretly to London to join some of their own friends for a party. Next day they left for France and spent three weeks cycling in Normandy.

After their honeymoon they settled in Paris. As Constance had inherited some money they rented a larger apartment and even had a maid, Josephine, who stayed with them for many years.

Late the following summer they returned to Ireland. Constance was expecting a baby and wanted it to be born at Lissadell. Her only child, a girl, was born on the 13 November 1901. They christened her Maeve after the great queen who, legend says, is buried on Knocknarea, the flat-topped mountain that overlooks the Gore-Booth's home.

As soon as Constance was well enough she and Casimir returned to Paris leaving Maeve with her grandmother. As she was only about twelve weeks old it was probably thought best to leave her in Sligo where a nanny had been engaged to look after her. This was to be the first of many long separations. Maeve who was adored by Lady Gore-Booth spent most of her childhood at Lissadell.

In May Casimir decided to take Constance to stay with his family on their estates in the Ukraine. She was excited about the trip and especially looked forward to meeting Casimir's family.

Constance was an immediate hit with her in-laws because of her easy-going manner and their mutual love of horses. Casimir's little boy Stanislas also liked her and later recalled her as being 'tall, slim and exquisite' and smelling of perfume, paint and cigarettes. He said she was 'as kind as she was beautiful'.

The Markieviczs lived in a large white house which overlooked paddocks full of grazing horses and wheatlands that stretched as far as the eye could see. Life on the Ukraine estate was similar to life at Lissadell. Constance fitted in well though she was a little surprised to find that some of the servants still slept outside their masters' doors at night. She noted too that the Russian peasants lived much like the Irish peasants in small cabins.

Constance loved her stay in the Ukraine and the summer slipped by in a round of hunting parties, picnics and painting. They left in October, before the winter snows came, promising to return the following summer.

In 1903 Casimir and Constance decided to move to Dublin and to bring Casi's son Stanislas, or 'Stasko' as he was called, to live with them. They went to the Ukraine again for a holiday and to collect the little boy. They also smuggled a young Polish Jew named Janko out of the country to save him from military service in the Russian army. Years later when Constance was trying to collect money for the wives and children of the 'lock-out' strikers Janko arrived at her door to give her a donation. He had never forgotten her earlier kindness to him.

The Markieviczs' arrival in Dublin must have been quite a spectacle as apart from Stasko, Janko and their French maid Josephine, the Count and Countess had sixty-four cases of furniture and belongings. Little Maeve joined them at their new home – St. Mary's, Frankfort Avenue, Rathgar, a suburb of Dublin.

They had been expected home. Earlier that year artist, poet and essayist, George Russell (A.E.) had written to a friend that 'the Gore-Booth girl, who married the Polish Count with the unspellable name is going to settle near Dublin about summertime'. He obviously looked forward to this because he added, 'as they are both clever it will create an art atmosphere. We might get the materials for a revolt, a new Irish art club.' But when the revolt came it was not in the art world.

While Constance had been in London and Paris many changes had been taking place in Ireland. In 1898 a Local Government Act had been passed setting up county and district councils in which, for the first time, Irish women were given the right to vote. Several land acts were passed in the late nineteenth century as a direct result of agitation by the Land League. These were known as the Land Purchase Acts. In 1903, the year Countess Markievicz returned to live in Dublin, the most important of the land acts, the Wyndham Land Act, was passed.

The Wyndham Act was a huge success. It changed the

Constance dressed for an evening in Dublin Castle.

face of Irish farming. Within a few years 300,000 tenant farmers had become owners of their land. A Department of Agriculture was set up to help improve farming methods. All these changes were part of the Conservative Government's policy of 'Killing Home Rule with kindness'. They believed that if they gave a little to the native Irish their leaders in Parliament would stop demanding Home Rule.

Other changes taking place came from the Irish themselves and covered all aspects of life. Dublin was bubbling over with creative energy and activity. People flocked to see the new plays by Yeats and John Millington Synge performed by the Irish National Theatre at the Abbey in Dublin. They learned Irish and the old Irish stories and poems at classes held by the Gaelic League and they went to see Irish sports like hurling at the Gaelic Athletic Association (G.A.A.) matches. Irish nationalists were printing their own newspapers filled with articles on Irish history and politics. All this newly awakened pride in Irish culture and traditions led to an out-pouring of artistic talent.

As artists, Constance and Casimir quickly became involved in the artistic life of the city. They soon made friends with A.E. who was a neighbour and in 1904, during Horse Show Week, the three of them held an art exhibition. The following year they set up the United Arts Club with Yeats and his brother Jack the painter, Synge, the painter William Orpen and the song-writer Percy French. The Arts Club still exists today in Fitzwilliam Square, Dublin.

Meanwhile the social life of the Dublin Castle set continued its merry whirl. Constance knew most of the people in this set and she and Casimir became frequent guests at balls and house parties. They were regular visitors to Dublin Castle and the Vice-Regal Lodge – home of the Viceroy.

INVOLVEMENT IN NATIONALISM

Constance was approaching her fortieth birthday and her life seemed firmly rooted among the Protestant Anglo-Irish but this was about to change completely.

Dublin then was a city of great contrasts. The rich lived in splendour in their big houses while the poor lived in squalor in some of the worst living conditions in Europe. It was impossible for someone of Constance's kind nature to ignore the poverty around her. Her friend Lady Fingall, attending a ball at Dublin Castle, described the view from a bedroom window: 'We can hear the music as we put last touches to our hair and our frocks in one of the bedrooms upstairs. The windows of that room look out on an appalling slum, a fact characteristic of the life of those days. But the windows are curtained and one need not lift the curtains.'

Most of the Castle set managed not to 'lift the curtains', they managed to ignore the misery around them. As time went on Constance began to feel that her life of balls, parties and amusements was meaningless and shallow when so many people around her had barely enough to eat.

She was thinking about these things when, in the summer of 1907, she rented a small whitewashed cottage in the Dublin mountains. Casi was in Poland visiting his family and Maeve was with her grandmother at Lissadell so Con and Stasko went to spend some weeks in the two-roomed cottage where Stasko could play in the countryside and Con could paint. Con soon became a well-loved figure among the local children because as she cycled around the lanes and byways she always had her pockets full of sweets for them.

The previous tenant in the cottage was the poet Padraig Colum. He had left a lot of newspapers behind – papers issued by nationalist organisations and written by people who believed the only solution to Ireland's problems was complete separation from England. They believed that only in a free Ireland, governed by Irish people, could the Irish gain prosperity and regain their pride in their own culture and heritage.

Constance spent many long summer evenings reading

While on holiday in a cottage in the Dublin mountains, Constance finds and reads some nationalist newspapers.

through these papers. They opened up a whole new world to her. She began to realise that part of the reason for Ireland's poverty was the fact that Ireland was governed by people far away in the Parliament in London. She too became convinced that the only way forward for Ireland was to become completely independent. As she read the historical articles she became aware of the continuing struggle for independence which had been fought by Hugh O'Neill, Wolfe Tone, Robert Emmet and the Fenians. She found out for the first time that there were groups of people in Dublin dedicated to continuing this struggle and she decided to seek them out and become involved.

POLITICAL LIFE

The main political party in Ireland at this time was the Home Rule party, or the Irish Parliamentary Party as it was also known, founded in 1870 and led by John Redmond. The Home Rule party wanted to re-establish a parliament in Dublin. Ireland had had a parliament of its own which met in what is now the Bank of Ireland opposite Trinity College in Dublin. But the British Government abolished this Parliament in 1801. After the 1798 rebellion the British were nervous of more uprisings and they decided it was safer to have Irish politicians sitting in the London Parliament at Westminster than in a parliament of their own in Dublin. Many Irish politicians disagreed. This had eventually led to the setting up of the Home Rule party. Its members didn't want complete separation from Britain; they were content for Ireland to remain part of the British Empire. They just wanted an Irish parliament to deal with local Irish affairs, while the big, international issues could still be decided in London.

A much smaller organisation, Sinn Féin, was led by Arthur Griffith. He was opposed to Redmond and the Home Rule party. Like many other young men of the time he had no faith in Redmond's party. The campaign for Home Rule had started forty years previously before most of these young men were born and had still not achieved its goals.

30

Griffith had no patience with Redmond's policy of waiting for the British Parliament to pass laws allowing Home Rule for Ireland. He believed that Members of Parliament elected by the Irish should simply refuse to sit in the British Parliament and should instead set up their own independent parliament in Dublin without waiting for British legislation. He was opposed to physical violence and believed these changes could be brought about peacefully.

One evening, shortly after her return from the cottage, Constance went to an 'at Home' in A.E.'s house. She spotted Arthur Griffith sitting in a corner and straightway went up to him and told him she wanted to join Sinn Féin. Griffith was astonished that this wealthy, Anglo-Irish woman would want to join his organisation. He immediately decided she must be a spy sent by Dublin Castle to report back on the activities of Sinn Féin. He put her off and suggested she might join the Gaelic League instead.

Constance was not the kind to be easily deterred. In March 1908, she accompanied Casi to the grand St. Patrick's Ball in Dublin Castle. It was her last appearance at a social function in the Castle. Soon after, in spite of Griffith's refusal, she began to attend Sinn Féin meetings and to get to know the members.

It took a lot of courage for someone of Constance's background to become involved with an organisation like Sinn Féin. All her relations and nearly all her friends were Unionists, that is they believed in the Union between Ireland and England. They would have considered Constance a traitor because she had joined with people who wanted to break the union and set up an independent Ireland.

One evening while she was attending a Sinn Féin meeting Constance met a young woman named Helena Moloney. Helena belonged to a nationalist women's organisation called Inghinidhe na hEireann (Daughters of Ireland). Maud Gonne had set up this group in 1900. The members believed that Ireland should be completely independent from England, and wished to spread this belief among Irish women. They also wanted Irish people to take pride in being Irish by encouraging the study of Irish language, literature, history and music. To help spread their beliefs they decided to bring out a newspaper called *Bean na hEireann*. Helena Moloney invited Constance to a meeting to discuss setting up this newspaper.

The meeting took place on a cold rainy evening. The members had all arrived when Helena told them that she had invited a new member, but there was no sign of the new recruit. Suddenly the door opened and in came Constance resplendent in evening dress, furs around her neck and diamonds in her hair. The other members who liked to dress simply in Irish-made clothes were all aghast. They thought Helena had made a mistake and invited one of the Castle set to their meeting. But Constance soon won them over and by the end of the meeting she had been elected onto the committee to organise the newspaper. When the newspaper came out later that year it had a cover designed by Constance.

Another friend she made during 1908 was a young man called Bulmer Hobson. He was Vice-President of Sinn Féin. Unlike Arthur Griffith, Bulmer Hobson liked and trusted Constance from the start. He arranged for her to become a member of the Drumcondra branch of Sinn Féin in November 1908.

In the same year Bulmer Hobson took Constance to meet Tom Clarke. Clarke had been involved in Fenian activities in the 1880s. The Fenians were a secret organisation dedicated to securing Irish independence and setting up an Irish Republic. Clarke had been arrested and spent fifteen years in prison before emigrating to the United States. He had returned to Ireland in 1907 and was now a member of the I.R.B. (Irish Republican Brotherhood) a secret organisation that carried on the beliefs and tradition of the Fenians. Unlike Arthur Griffith, the members of the I.R.B. believed that an independent Ireland could only be achieved through an armed struggle.

When Clarke returned to Ireland he had set up a small

tobacconist's shop in Parnell Street which had soon become a popular meeting place for nationalists. It was to this shop that Bulmer Hobson brought Constance. She was very impressed by Tom Clarke, this kind man who had suffered so much. 'What you got from him,' she wrote, was 'interest in your schemes, encouragement for your hopes, support in your hours of despair.'

THE FIANNA

By the end of 1908 Constance had already travelled a long way on the road that had opened up before her during her summer holiday of 1907. However, her life was not totally taken up by these new elements. These were years of great activity in the theatre in Dublin. Casimir and Constance knew all the leading people involved in the world of drama – Yeats, A.E. and others. Casimir now became involved in acting and producing plays. He set up a drama company and put on several plays at Yeats's new theatre – the Abbey. Constance took the leading role in many of them and enjoyed herself immensely.

But Constance and Casimir were beginning to drift apart. Though they remained very good friends and enjoyed their shared involvement in the theatre their interests were leading them in different directions.

Casimir sympathised with Constance's new activities in Sinn Féin and the Daughters of Ireland, but he didn't want to get caught up in nationalist politics. He was happy to be involved with the dramatic and artistic life of Dublin, after that he just wanted to have a good time. He referred to Constance good-humouredly as 'my floating landmine' because of her increasing commitment to ending British rule in Ireland.

In March 1909 Constance heard that the Viceroy had set up a troop of boy scouts in Dublin. She realised immediately that these young boys would be taught to be proud of the fact that they were part of the British Empire. They would be taught to take pride in the traditions and history of the British Empire instead of those of Ireland.

Constance and the Fianna boys set off for scout camp, their luggage piled onto the donkey's cart.

She wrote later: 'Surely nothing could be sadder than to see the sons of men who had thrown in their lot with the Fenians ... saluting the flag that flew in triumph over every defeat their nation has known ... I could see these children growing to manhood and gaily enlisting in the British Army or Police forces and being used to batter their own class into submission.'

Constance was never happy just to complain about things. She set about doing something. She decided the best way to undermine the Viceroy's boy scouts was to set up a rival organisation. At the next Sinn Féin meeting she suggested that Sinn Féin should establish an organisation for young boys that was totally Irish in character. Arthur Griffith wasn't interested in the idea. Undaunted, Constance went ahead and set up a group herself. Her friend, Helena Moloney, supported her idea and said she would help. They decided to call the new organisation the Red Branch Knights. Their first recruits were eight boys from the National School in Brunswick Street. The first few meetings were spent learning drill, signalling and other scouting activities. Then they decided to go on camp up the Dublin mountains.

They set off in great excitement with all their equipment piled into a cart drawn by a small pony. As Constance later wrote, 'We knew a little valley away up on the side of the Three Rock Mountain, with a little stream bubbling through it and a lovely carpet of soft, close-cropped grass ... After long hours of pushing, pulling, lifting, resting and pushing again, we arrived at the last gate at the end of the track. We started to pitch the tents on a grassy slope where the hill slid down to the stream. It took a long, long time ... Tents are very hard to pitch if you don't know how, especially at night ... Next comes the task of trying to disentangle jam from blankets, frying-pans, cushions, poetry books and all the other indispensable articles we had brought. Candles were the only important thing we had forgotten. But at last everything had found a place, the boys were comfortably settled, and we turned in and drifted into dream-land to the tuneful accompaniment of the snores of the six boys in the other tent.'

Constance, Helena and the boys spent two very happy days in camp and on the evening of the third day packed up to go home. They had one more difficulty in store. The pony had enjoyed his freedom so much that they had to chase him around the field for a long time before they could catch him to harness him up again.

Constance was delighted the boys had enjoyed the trip so much. She was now full of plans to expand the group, and her friend Bulmer Hobson agreed to help her. She decided she would hold a public meeting to attract more recruits. She rented a hall in Camden Street and put an ad in the paper asking for boys 'willing to work for the independence of Ireland'. About a hundred boys turned up. Her new organisation was now firmly established. At Bulmer Hobson's request she changed the name from the Red Branch Knights to the Fianna, a band of elite warriors in ancient Ireland.

It was then that Constance's ability to shoot well became important. She bought rifles and trained the boys to shoot. Like many others at this time Constance had come to the conclusion that England would never allow Ireland to become independent by peaceful means. She believed that the Irish Republic she dreamed of would only become a reality through an armed struggle. She wanted her Fianna boys to be ready to take part in this struggle when they were young men.

Many of the Fianna boys came from poor families who lived in dreadful conditions in the Dublin slums. Constance believed it would be very good for them to spend some time in the healthy fresh air of the countryside. In the summer of 1910, while Casi was in Poland, Con and her friends Helena and Bulmer Hobson rented a twelve-bedroomed house with large gardens just outside Dublin, in what is now Raheny. Con and Helena moved in with the Fianna boys, and Constance hired a gardener to cultivate the land and train the boys how to grow fruit and vegetables so that they could produce all their food themselves. Unfortunately, Con and Helena had to be away a lot of the time and the boys, left to themselves, preferred to roam the countryside rather than work in the garden, so very little got done.

The summer passed and eventually Casi returned from Poland. He has left us an amusing account of his arrival at his new home in Belcamp House: 'I have great trouble to find this house but at last I find it and I send away the cabby. I find the house at the end of the avenue, all dark, all silent. I knock and knock but not a sound. I go around the back and I call out "Constance". No sound. I come around to the front and I knock and call out "Constance". After a while a dirty little ragamuffin puts his head out and say, "Who da?" I say, "I want to see Countess Markievicz!" He go away and I wait. No sound. I knock again and I call "Constance!" Another window go up and another dirty little ragamuffin say, "Who da?" I say, "I am Count Markievicz and I want to see Countess Markievicz." I hear much scuffling and running and at last the door open. It is all dark but I see Constance. "It's very dark, Constance," I say. "We have only one lamp," she says, "and the gardener is reading with that." That is how I return to my home.'

Casi was appalled when he realised the amount of money Constance was spending on running the household especially as no money was coming in from the land. He frightened the gardener so much with his demands for explanations that the poor man went out and cut down a holly tree. He sold this for £1.50 to show he could contribute some money to the project. His gesture only made matters worse as the angry landlord of the house demanded £5 compensation from Constance for the tree!

After much discussion Constance reluctantly agreed that the experiment was a failure. Eventually they found a new tenant for the house and moved back into Dublin.

Although the Raheny project had failed, the Fianna were going from strength to strength. A young recruit named Liam Mellowes took on the job of cycling all over the country telling people about the Fianna and setting up new branches. The boys were devoted to Constance. From this time on there were always Fianna boys living in her home and the people of Dublin became used to the sight of Constance going from place to place surrounded by boys of ten years of age upwards. Casi was not too pleased with this invasion of his home. He called them 'sprouts' because they sprouted everywhere, under his bed, beneath his chairs, inside cupboards, 'and the little devil sprouts', he said 'drink whiskey, even locked whiskey'.

In 1911 two occasions arose which gave Con the opportunity of showing publicly what she thought of British rule in Ireland. After the death of the British king there was a period of mourning. Everybody was expected to dress in black while attending public functions. At the theatre one evening, everyone was soberly dressed in black when, just before the curtain went up and much to the audience's consternation, Constance swept in defiantly dressed in a gown of bright red velvet.

Later on that year when big crowds had turned out in Dublin to welcome the new king and queen, Constance, with a friend of hers, The O'Rahilly, hung a huge banner across the bottom of Grafton Street which read 'Thou art not conquered yet dear Land'.

In 1912 Constance moved into a house called Surrey House in Rathmines. The locals nicknamed it 'Scurry House' because of the constant activity and coming and going at the house. Constance was recklessly generous by nature and her house was open to anyone in trouble, to anyone who needed a meal or a bed for the night. There was always room there, especially for her devoted Fianna boys.

POVERTY IN DUBLIN

It was also in 1912 that, with her friends Maud Gonne, Helena Moloney, the Gifford sisters and Tom Clarke's wife Kathleen, Constance set up a food kitchen in two national schools in the city centre area. They served over 250 meals

*Big Jim Larkin addresses a Labour
meeting in Dublin.*

a day to children, most of whom would otherwise have had
nothing to eat all day. Though Constance didn't know it
then, this experience in preparing food for large numbers
was to prove very valuable in the near future.

Constance had by now experienced the squalor and
poverty in which many Dubliners lived by visiting the
homes of her Fianna boys. The population of Dublin then
was only 400,000 but more than 87,000 of this number
lived in what were called 'tenements'.

Tenements were houses that had been built for the rich in the eighteenth century. These families had then moved either to England, as a result of the abolition of the Irish Parliament, or to the suburbs of Dublin. The houses they left behind were rented out to the poor room by room. Most families lived in just one room – sometimes as many as six or seven people per family. The houses were cold and damp and generally in bad repair. There would usually be thirty to forty people in one house with just one toilet in the backyard and one cold water tap. These families had very few possessions. Many used boxes for furniture and slept on straw. Their meals consisted of bread and tea twice a day and potatoes with maybe cabbage or onions for dinner. Because of these terrible living conditions, illness spread rapidly and the death of babies and young children was a common occurrence.

The worst thing was that the families could see no hope of ever escaping from their desperate situation. Because there were more people looking for work than there were jobs available, the employers could always find workers to fill the jobs. Most of these people were employed on a 'casual' basis, that is, they had to turn up every day to see if there was work for them. Some days there was but other days they were sent away. When they didn't work they got no money as there was no system of dole.

There appeared in Dublin at this time a man who was to bring hope to the poor. His name was Jim Larkin, known to his friends as 'Big Jim'. His statue stands today in O'Connell Street, opposite Clery's department store. He was appalled by the misery of Dublin's poor and decided to do something about it. He was a large powerful man and his fiery speeches inspired hope and courage in the hearts of the poor. Constance met him for the first time in 1910 when he was addressing a meeting and she described the effect he had on her and the workers: 'He forced his own self-reliance and self-respect on them. From that day I looked upon Larkin as a friend and was out to do any little thing I could do to help him.'

In 1909 Larkin had founded a union called the ITGWU (The Irish Transport and General Workers' Union). Its aim was to get employers to improve the wages and working conditions of their workers. By 1913 thousands of workers had joined Larkin's union. The employers began to get nervous about 'Larkinism' as they called the trade union movement. They didn't want to give in to the union's demands. In June 1913 they formed their own association, the Dublin Employers' Federation, to organise opposition to Larkin. William Martin Murphy was the head of this organisation. The employers decided they would not employ anybody who belonged to the ITGWU and they asked their workers to sign a document promising they would never join the union. Most workers refused and the employers then locked them out, that is they refused to allow them to work. Soon 25,000 people were out of work. The employers had decided to starve the workers into submission.

Larkin continued to address huge meetings of workers outside his union's headquarters at Liberty Hall, a building which occupied the same site as the modern Liberty Hall of today. The authorities and the police considered Larkin a troublemaker and decided to put an end to his activities. He had planned a meeting to take place in O'Connell Street on Sunday 29 August 1913. A few days before it was due the police banned the meeting. When Larkin was informed of this, he publicly burned the police document banning the meeting in front of a large crowd and told the people 'I will be in Sackville Street [the name by which O'Connell Street was known then] on Sunday next, dead or alive, and if I am dead I hope you will carry me there.'

The police immediately issued a warrant for his arrest but Constance took him into hiding in Surrey House. The problem was, how could he fulfill his promise to appear at the meeting on Sunday? In Surrey House, Casi, Con, Jim, Helena Moloney and the young Gifford sisters discussed the problem. As usual it didn't take long for Constance to come up with an idea. They decided to dress Larkin up as an elderly clergyman and smuggle him into the Imperial Hotel which had a balcony looking out onto O'Connell Street. Better still, the hotel was owned by William Martin Murphy. The conspirators enjoyed the joke of outwitting the authorities in the enemies' own territory.

The next morning Constance powdered Big Jim's hair until it was grey and dressed him up in a top hat and false beard. He approached the hotel with the stooped, slow walk of an elderly gentleman and was helped in by one of the porters. There was a small crowd waiting in the street, wondering whether Big Jim would keep his promise. Suddenly they saw the balcony door of the Imperial Hotel being flung open and the tall, erect figure they knew well walked out. He started to speak and the cheering crowd surged forward to listen. He just had time to tell them he had kept his promise before the police raced in and arrested him. As Big Jim emerged from the hotel escorted by the police, Constance stood beside him and called for three cheers from the crowd. She was immediately struck in the face by a police baton. This was the signal for the police in the street to attack the crowd.

What happened next has been described by a woman who was there on the day: 'A lad beside me yelled, "Hey! The peelers [policemen] have drawn their batons." The next thing I knew the peelers were upon us. All you could hear was the thud, thump, crack of the batons as they fell on the heads of the crowd ... The peelers came steadily like mowing machines, and behind them the street was like a battlefield dotted with bodies. Some of them still lying twisting in pain.' By the end of the day hundreds of people were being treated in hospital as a result of police brutality.

The police also arrested another ITGWU leader, a friend of Larkin's, James Connolly. Like Larkin, Connolly was angered by the atrocious living and working conditions of the poor. He wrote: 'Dublin is infamous for the perfectly hellish conditions under which its people are housed and

'Three cheers for Big Jim,' Constance cried as he was arrested and taken away.

under which its men and women labour for a living.' Connolly believed that Ireland should be independent from England too, but he thought it would take many years before this could be achieved. In the meantime he dedicated his life to trying to improve the lives of the poor. He had no time for nationalists like Arthur Griffith who devoted all their energies to working for an independent Ireland while ignoring the misery of the poor around them.

During 1913, through their work for the ITGWU, Constance and James Connolly became very close friends. Connolly's home and family were in Belfast so when in Dublin he stayed with Constance in Surrey House.

Larkin was released from prison on 12 September 1913. His immediate concern was to provide food for the 25,000 locked-out workers and their families. Larkin organised for food and money to be sent over by the sympathetic trade unions in England.

Large food kitchens were set up in Liberty Hall and Constance was put in charge of cooking and distributing food to thousands of workers and their families. She had a large group of volunteer helpers and they worked from morning to night peeling huge mounds of potatoes, chopping vegetables, scraping bones and making gallons of soup. All day long the poor queued outside Liberty Hall with tins, jars or whatever containers they could find to take away the precious nourishment.

During 1913 there were constant attacks by police on striking workers and on union meetings. As a result of these attacks Larkin decided to set up an armed force to protect the workers. He called the force the Irish Citizen Army. The day-to-day running of the Citizen Army was looked after by an army council. Constance was treasurer of the council and the council secretary was Seán O'Casey. O'Casey was later to become a world famous dramatist. He disliked and mistrusted Constance. Because of her wealthy background and upper-class accent he didn't believe she was sincere in her attitude to the poor. In spite of the long hours she spent working in the kitchen at

Liberty Hall he later wrote that she was just looking for attention and only worked when a member of the press was present. Of course this was untrue but unfortunately for Constance, while she was loved and admired by many, there were always people like O'Casey who felt uneasy with her and resented her because of her aristocratic accent and way of doing things.

The weary months of October and November 1913 rolled on and still there was no sign of the employers giving in. It was a bitterly cold winter and the spirits of the workers sank lower and lower. Christmas came and went and the situation worsened. The money and food coming from England was now reduced to a trickle. The people were in despair. Gradually, during January 1914, the workers started drifting back to work, signing the employers' anti-union document. By the end of February it was all over. Most of the workers had gone back. The miseries they had suffered during the terrible winter of 1913 seemed to have been in vain. Connolly wrote, 'So we Irish workers must go down into Hell and eat the dust of defeat and betrayal.'

In spite of appearances the struggle had not been for nothing. Many employers had lost a lot of money during the Lock Out and they were scared by the determination the workers had shown. As 1914 progressed many workers rejoined the Union and the employers took no action. They didn't want a repeat of the troubles of 1913.

THE HOME RULE STRUGGLE

While Constance and the trade unionists had been involved in the fight for workers' rights, there had also been great political activity. In 1912 the House of Commons of the British Parliament agreed to grant Home Rule to Ireland. The announcement was welcomed by nationalists but Unionists were shocked at the prospect of being ruled by a Dublin parliament. Most Unionists lived in Ulster and they decided to fight against the introduction of Home Rule to Ireland.

Edward Carson was the leader of the Ulster Unionists

and he pledged to use 'all means necessary to defeat Home Rule'. In 1913 he set up an armed force called the Ulster Volunteers and a provisional government to take control of Ulster from the day Home Rule came into force. Faced with this opposition the British Prime Minister, Herbert Asquith, and the Home Rule movement leader, John Redmond, became nervous and began to back down from their original idea of Home Rule for all Ireland. The nationalists were outraged when they saw their dream of a Dublin parliament legislating for the whole of Ireland fading. They in turn set up a force called the Irish Volunteers to defend Home Rule. A women's section called Cumann na mBan was also established.

The Home Rule Bill was signed into law by King George V on 18 September 1914. But the whole idea of Home Rule was shelved when World War I broke out in 1914. Redmond, in a speech in Co. Wicklow, urged the Volunteers to support Britain in the war against Germany. Following Germany's invasion of Belgium, he told them, it was their duty to fight 'for the freedom of small nations'. Most of the 180,000 Volunteers followed his call and joined the British Army.

Only 11,000 men now remained in the Irish Volunteers. They were opposed to Redmond's policies and refused to fight on behalf of Britain. The leaders of this group were Professor Eoin MacNeill, Bulmer Hobson, The O'Rahilly, Patrick Pearse, Joseph Plunkett, and Thomas MacDonagh. The plans Pearse, Plunkett and MacDonagh had for the Volunteers were quite different from those of John Redmond.

O'DONOVAN-ROSSA'S FUNERAL

Early in 1915 Constance was honoured by the ITGWU. At a special ceremony in Liberty Hall she was presented with a decorated manuscript by the members of the Union for her 'unselfish and earnest labours' on their behalf during the Great Dublin Lock-Out. They also made her an honorary member of the union – a rare recognition for a woman in those days. These two acts of friendship and affection delighted Con.

Constance's whole life had by now become devoted to advancing the cause of Irish nationalism and helping Dublin's poor. Casi found this more and more difficult to cope with. His home was always full of people agitating for some political or social cause. Money was scarce because of Con's reckless generosity to the poor. He must often have longed for the old days when he and Con belonged to the Castle set and lived a life of gracious ease and pleasure. Finally in December 1913 he decided to leave Ireland for a while and he set off to work in the Balkans as a newspaper correspondent.

For many months Con had no word from him. Finally in April a long-awaited letter arrived. In it Casi described how, when the war started, he had ridden more than 1100 kilometres on horseback to the Ukraine to join an Imperial Hussar Cavalry regiment. He went on to relate that he had been wounded in battle and was now back on his family estates and wanted Stasko to join him there. Con, who had always had a great affection for the boy, was very upset. When Stasko left she feared she would never see him or Casi again as the war was still raging in Europe. With Maeve now living permanently in Lissadell, her family was completely broken up.

Alone now, she threw herself even more feverishly into the Irish causes. She became more militant and longed for an armed struggle in Ireland. With this in mind she drilled and trained her Fianna boys in the art of soldiery. She took them up to remote parts of the Dublin mountains to give them target practice. Con taught her boys so well that some of the older Fianna were secretly passing on their skills to members of the I.R.B. When not with the Fianna she was out training with the Citizen Army. Led by Connolly and Constance the Citizen Army was a familiar sight in the streets of Dublin carrying out manoeuvres and route marches. One evening they even had the audacity to stage a mock attack on Dublin Castle, much to the astonishment of the sentries on duty there. For Connolly it was a kind of trial run.

Constance's home became 'open house' for nationalists of all shades of opinion. They ranged from pacifists like Francis and Hannah Sheehy-Skeffington to Connolly, who was openly preaching insurrection in his newspaper *The Workers' Republic*. In spite of the fact that the house was often watched by the police the evening gatherings at Surrey House were great fun. At the drop of a hat the carpet was rolled back and singing and dancing would commence amidst Con's fine furniture and beautiful pictures. There was a lot of political talk too and many later remembered the night a young Volunteer called Michael Collins recited Robert Emmet's speech from the dock to a hushed room. A French visitor who spent an evening at Surrey House wrote afterwards that it was like visiting a military headquarters.

In May 1915 Sir Edward Carson and seven other Unionists were invited to join a new coalition government in London. This news shocked the Home Rulers as it meant the Unionists now had power to decide the fate of Home Rule. From that time on even moderate Irishmen knew that Home Rule was doomed and many flocked to join the Irish Volunteers.

Those like Clarke and Constance who wanted nothing less than full independence for Ireland saw this as their chance to win people over to their way of thinking. All they needed was an opportunity to rouse public opinion. The chance they were looking for came late that summer when a famous old Fenian Jeremiah O'Donovan-Rossa died in America. As he wished to be buried in Ireland, his body was brought home. A big funeral was arranged and all the nationalist organisations, including the small band of men and women who made up the Citizen Army, took part in the procession. Thousands lined the street to watch the funeral go past. Constance's sister, Eva, and Esther Roper, who were on a visit to Dublin, watched Constance and her little army march past. Afterwards Esther remarked, 'Well

Rebels shooting from the rooftops of Dublin during the 1916 Rising.

thank goodness, they simply can't be planning a rising now, not with such a tiny force.'

But Eva and Esther had not gone to Glasnevin Cemetery where Tom Clarke had arranged for Patrick Pearse, whom he knew to be a good orator, to speak at the grave side. Pearse, a member of the I.R.B., gave an impassioned and chilling speech ending: 'They think they have pacified Ireland. Think they have foreseen everything ... but the fools, the fools, they have left us our Fenian dead and while Ireland holds these graves, Ireland unfree will never be at peace.' Pearse's words inspired all who heard them.

PLANNING A REBELLION

Esther Roper was wrong – a rising was being planned. As soon as war broke out some of the Irish Volunteer leaders started plotting insurrection, believing that 'England's difficulty was Ireland's opportunity'. This group was led by Tom Clarke and included Patrick Pearse, Seán MacDermott, Eamon Ceannt, Joseph Mary Plunkett and Thomas MacDonagh. Together they formed the Military Council of the I.R.B. Secrecy was of the utmost importance to them, as all the earlier rebellions in Ireland had been betrayed by informers. Not even Eoin MacNeill, the leader of the Volunteers, knew of the plot or that the date for the rising, Easter Sunday 1916, had been decided.

The leaders sent a man called Roger Casement to Germany to seek arms, ammunition and, if possible, men to support the rising. Casement, an Irishman, had been knighted for his work in the British Colonial Service. He had returned to Ireland to rest because his health had suffered in the African colonies and through his friendship with Bulmer Hobson became involved with the Irish nationalists.

Connolly, helped by Michael Mallin, his second-in-command, and Constance, was laying his own plans for a workers' revolution which he hoped would lead to the setting up of a socialist republic. To help them a young friend from Glasgow, called Margaret Skinnider, smuggled detonators into the country when she came to spend Christmas at Surrey House. Con and herself went off to the Wicklow mountains to practice using them and were thrilled when they managed to blow up a wall.

Through their network of spies the I.R.B. learned of Connolly's plans. In order to stop him they told him about the rising. They had to trust him as they feared a workers' revolt before Easter Sunday would ruin all their carefully laid plans. He agreed to wait and join with them.

In the meantime he continued to defy the authorities by printing blatantly rebellious articles in his paper. This led to a police raid on Liberty Hall. Fortunately they confiscated only some of the newspapers but Connolly knew they would be back and that next time they might find the printing press and large store of arms hidden in the basement. He decided to guard the building day and night. As an officer, Constance took her turn at sentry duty.

The question of what to wear posed a problem for the women of the Citizen Army – should it be skirts or trousers? In 1916, women in Ireland did not wear pants so to avoid causing outrage most of the women decided on skirts. Nora Connolly described Con at the time as looking every inch a soldier in a dark green woollen tunic with brass buttons, green tweed knee-breeches, black stockings and heavy boots with a bandolier slung across her shoulder. The whole outfit was set off by her best black hat complete with its plume of cock feathers. She wore a skirt over her breeches when out marching so as to avoid attracting attention but was quite sure that breeches would be much more practical for military purposes. Constance had a similar uniform made for Margaret Skinnider who was due to return to Dublin for Easter week. She too was given knee-breeches because she was going to be a bicycle dispatch rider when the fateful day came.

It was quite extraordinary for a woman to be a military officer in the early part of this century. But Constance was not only in the army but also a commissioned officer with the rank of lieutenant. She carried arms and held partial command.

On the Monday before Easter the rebels secretly set up the Provisional Government of the Irish Republic. They wrote a proclamation which Connolly had printed in Liberty Hall. The seven leaders, Clarke, MacDermott, Pearse, Connolly, MacDonagh, Ceannt and Plunkett signed it.

PERSUADING MACNEILL

Just one major obstacle remained – that was persuading Eoin MacNeill, the leader of the Irish Volunteers, to join them. MacNeill was a moderate opposed to rebellion and he had said he would only resist if the British tried to disarm the Volunteers. As the Ulster Volunteers had been allowed to keep their arms he did not think this would happen. He believed the Irish people did not want a rising and he knew one would have no chance of success against the well-trained and well-armed British forces.

On the Tuesday of Easter week, MacNeill was told that a German ship, the *Aud*, was due to arrive in Kerry laden with arms and, more importantly, he was shown a letter alleging that the Government was about to arrest all the leaders of the Irish Volunteers. This letter, known as the 'Castle document', was probably forged by some members of the I.R.B. Military Council to sway MacNeill. It did. He gave the order to resist.

Three days later, on Good Friday, things went disastrously wrong. The *Aud* arrived too early and was captured by the British. Unknown to the Germans the British had deciphered their secret war code and were lying in wait for the ship in Fenit harbour. The *Aud* was escorted to Cobh where the captain, having disembarked with his crew, scuttled the boat. Casement, who had come to Ireland separately by submarine, was arrested shortly after landing at Banna Strand. When MacNeill heard the news he decided to call off the rising. With no arms and the British on the alert he believed they would all be massacred. On Easter Saturday night he placed an announcement in the newspapers saying: 'All orders given to the Irish Volunteers for tomorrow, Easter Sunday are rescinded ...'

The change of orders caused great confusion. When Constance read the announcement on Easter Sunday morning she was stunned. She raced down to Liberty Hall to ask Connolly what had happened and he replied 'MacNeill has cut the ground from under our feet ...' The Military Council met later that day at Liberty Hall and decided to go ahead with the rising next day. There was a frenzy of activity at the Hall as new orders were sent out. Constance said later that Easter Sunday 1916, was 'the busiest day I ever lived through'. She was so tired that night that when she was unloading her pistol she accidently sent a bullet through the bedroom door.

THE EASTER RISING

Easter Monday dawned bright and sunny. The leaders arrived at Liberty Hall not knowing whether their new orders would be obeyed and MacNeill's notice ignored. Four battalions, consisting of about 1,600 men, did arrive and lined up in front of the Hall. After a bugle had sounded fall-in they marched away. The rising had begun. The main group of Volunteers wheeled into O'Connell Street and headed for the General Post Office (G.P.O.), occupied it and hoisted the Irish tricolour on the roof. Then, to the astonishment of passersby, Pearse read out the Proclamation of the Republic in front of the building.

Meanwhile Constance, who had just learned to drive, loaded up a car with medical supplies and drove off to City Hall where Dr Kathleen Lynn was setting up a field hospital. Dr Lynn had trained the Citizen Army recruits in first aid. Having dropped the supplies she motored on to St. Stephen's Green to join Mallin. By the time she arrived he had taken over the park – much to the annoyance of the public. He was glad to see Con as he knew she was a crack shot and would be invaluable as a sniper when the fighting started. They hadn't long to wait.

Once the Castle, which the rebels had failed to take,

Hoisting the tricolour on the roof of the College of Surgeons.

recovered from the shock of the surprise attack, the British military were moved into position. St. Stephen's Green was overlooked on all sides by tall buildings so the rebels were quickly pinned down. There was no alternative for them but to retreat across the road to the College of Surgeons. Con and Margaret Skinnider were in the group assigned the task of taking over the College. Luckily, just as they darted across the street, the porter opened the door to a passerby and they were able to overpower him and gain entry. Once inside they rushed up to the roof and hoisted a tricolour from the flagpole for all to see. Gradually the rest of the unit escaped from the Green to join them. While in the park the rebels suffered many casualties.

The leaders in the G.P.O. fared little better as the army bombarded them from armoured cars and a gunboat, the *Helga*, which they brought up the Liffey. Buildings crumbled and caught fire, trapping the rebels. They held out for several days but on Saturday, 19 April 1916, they surrendered to prevent further bloodshed and destruction.

At the College of Surgeons Constance and Mallin were holding their own. All week long they kept the army at bay. As the army tightened the cordon around them, many were killed and injured. Margaret Skinnider was among the badly wounded. By Saturday night, unaware of their leaders' surrender, they were preparing to withstand another barrage. By now they had little ammunition left. As they expected this to be their last stand they gathered together and prayed for the dead and dying. The peace and tranquillity that descended on her comrades after the prayers had a lasting effect on Constance.

On Sunday morning an eerie silence descended on the streets. They wondered what was happening and wished they had some news about how their fellow rebels were doing in other parts of the city. They were about to send out a scout when a British officer arrived with Connolly's order to surrender. Many were angry and thought it was a trick but Constance said, 'I trust Connolly, we must obey.' Then Commandant Mallin and Lieutenant Markie-

Lieutenant Markievicz surrenders.

vicz surrendered. Constance, in a dramatic gesture, kissed her gun before handing it to the officer.

The officer, who was married to a kinswoman of Con's, offered to drive her to the Castle but she refused saying she wished to march there with her men. On the way Mallin and herself discussed their fate – would they be shot or hanged? The little band of rebels was jeered as it marched down Grafton Street and as it passed Trinity College an elderly man shouted 'shoot everyone of them'. In the Castle yard the rebels were loaded on to army trucks and taken to Kilmainham Jail. There Constance was separated from her comrades and put in solitary confinement. The rising was over and the centre of Dublin lay in ruins.

DEATH SENTENCE AND THE EXECUTIONS

British Government reaction was swift. They sent Major-General Sir John Maxwell, a tough high-ranking officer, over to take command. He was given a free hand to deal with the situation. He placed the country under martial law and rounded up thousands, including many innocent people, and sent them to prison camps in England. Irish reaction was just as strong. The Dublin people blamed the rebels for causing chaos, death and destruction in the city and were glad the rising had been quelled. On their way to the boats the prisoners were pelted with mud, mocked and jeered.

The leaders, including Constance, were court martialled in secret and sentenced to death. But Constance's death sentence was commuted to penal servitude for life because she was a woman. Eamon de Valera was also saved, probably because he was an American citizen. The others were not so lucky.

At dawn on 3 May Patrick Pearse, Tom Clarke and Thomas MacDonagh were taken out to the yard in Kilmainham Jail and shot. The next day Edward Daly, Michael O'Hanrahan, Willie Pearse (Patrick's younger brother) and Joseph Plunkett were executed. Of these four only Plunkett had signed the Proclamation and he was dying anyway from TB. On the eve of his execution he married Grace Gifford in prison.

On 5 May John MacBride, Maud Gonne's husband, was shot. On 8 May Con Colbert, Michael Mallin, Eamon Ceannt and Sean Heuston faced the firing squad. Heuston and Colbert were two of Con's Fianna boys. On 9 May Thomas Kent was executed in Cork.

On 11 May John Dillon, deputy leader of the Home Rule Party, made his famous speech in the House of Commons. Dillon wanted the executions to stop. He warned the Government that by 'letting loose a river of blood' in Dublin they were wiping out the life work of the Home Rule party.

It made no difference. The next day James Connolly and Sean MacDermott were shot. Connolly was strapped to a chair for his execution. He was unable to stand because of his wounds. Like the others shot in Kilmainham, they were buried in quicklime. Major-General Maxwell promised they would be the last. But by then it was too late, public opinion had changed.

It was the secrecy that surrounded the courts-martial and the executions more than anything else that brought about the change. Wild rumours spread through the city because no-one knew what was really happening. Lady Fingall said the daily shootings were 'like a continuous trickle of blood coming from under a locked door'. The news that Connolly had been brought to Kilmainham on a stretcher and then tied to a chair for his execution, horrified and sickened people. These events and the sense-less arrest and shooting of the harmless pacifist Francis Sheehy Skeffington and many other innocent people did what the rising had failed to do – swung the Irish nation behind the rebels.

MOUNTJOY JAIL

After her reprieve Constance was moved across the city to Mountjoy Jail. Her sister Eva and Esther Roper hurried over from England to see her. As they passed through the city every newspaper headline announced 'James Con-

*Burnt-out buildings and rubble on O'Connell Street
after the Rising.*

nolly shot this morning.' In Mountjoy Con asked almost
immediately whether Connolly had been shot. Eva couldn't
answer, as in return for a visitor's permit to see Con, she
had to promise not to mention politics. There was no need
for a reply, 'for with tears running slowly down her cheeks,'
Con said, 'you needn't tell me, I know. Why didn't they let
me die with my friends?' Then, recovering her composure,
she defiantly added, 'Well, Ireland was free for a week.'

For the next few weeks Constance remained in solitary confinement, though she obviously had some sympathisers in Mountjoy as news about her trickled out. This worried Major-General Maxwell who wrote to the Home Office in London, 'that the Countess Markievicz should be removed from Mountjoy Prison, Dublin, to some prison in England ... This lady is the only prisoner convicted for rebellion who is now in Ireland.'

Since the rising Con had become a heroic figure to the Irish and Maxwell feared she might escape and become a symbol of resistance so he decided to send her to Aylesbury Prison in England. Just before she left, Con managed to get a note, scribbled on toilet paper, smuggled out and sent to Eva telling her the news and asking her to try to see her in England. She also wrote that she was very relieved to hear from a friend that Maeve was more amused than shocked to learn that her mother was a convict.

Constance found Aylesbury a tough harsh cold place. She was put in with the most hardened prisoners because she had been convicted of treason. Con didn't mind the hard labour but the food was appalling and her health suffered. Her weight dropped from eighty kilos down to fifty-four kilos. One day she was so hungry she stole a turnip and ate it raw. She wrote to Eva that Aylesbury was a 'queer and lonely' place after Mountjoy, where the familiar sounds of the Dublin paperboys and children splashing in the nearby canal had been a consolation. As a joke she signed her letter 'Con(vict) 12'. The other awful aspect of Aylesbury for Con was its lack of hygiene. There were few washing facilities and lice and fleas crawled all over the inmates.

In December 1916 Lloyd George, then Prime Minister, granted an amnesty to the Irish internees. These men and women, who had been jeered and heckled when they were sent to English prisons just six months earlier, now returned as heroes and heroines. They were greeted by large cheering crowds. However Constance, a convicted rebel, was kept in jail. She had a lonely Christmas.

But Con had not been forgotten. Her friends in Ireland were continuously petitioning for better conditions for her. In her absence she was elected President of Cumann na mBan. With all the leaders of Sinn Féin either dead or in prison it was left to the women to keep the movement alive. Immediately after the rising, Nora Connolly, Nellie Gifford and Margaret Skinnider, recovered from her wounds, went to the United States to seek support for an Irish Republic and help for the prisoners. They found the Americans fascinated that a 'Countess' was among the leaders of the rising and the women made great use of Constance's death sentence and reprieve in their lectures.

She had support in Dublin too. Father Ryan from Church Street has described how the people in his area adored Con because she had come there many times 'to assist personally the poor and destitute'. If her spirits sagged they were lifted by a most unlikely friend, a tough Irish American girl called 'Chicago May'. May, a fellow prisoner in Aylesbury, was doing hard labour for a serious crime. She greatly admired Constance and later wrote of her: 'She was a real Irish patriot, sacrificing money, position, health and freedom for liberty.'

FREE AGAIN

After the rising the political mood changed in Ireland. With the swing to nationalism the British Prime Minister, Lloyd George, tried desperately to stem the tide. He offered Home Rule for Ireland in a limited form. Under pressure from Carson, who was a member of his cabinet, he changed the provisions of the 1914 Act to exclude Unionist Ulster. The offer was rejected by the Home Rule party. It was the beginning of the end for them. In the first by-election of 1917 the Home Rule party lost a seat to Count Plunkett, Joseph's father, who was supported by Arthur Griffith and Sinn Féin. This was no fluke. The Irish people showed that Home Rule no longer mattered to them when they voted

Conditions in prison were harsh, Constance lost a lot of weight and her health suffered.

in Sinn Féin candidates in the next three by-elections.

This dramatic change in attitude happened while Constance was in prison. When she was finally released in June 1917, fourteen months after her arrest, she could hardly believe the rapturous welcome she received in Dublin. Enormous crowds turned out to greet her. Traffic stopped, lamp posts were bedecked with tricolours and work was abandoned as the huge procession, led by a pipe band, slowly made its way through the cheering crowds to the ruins of Liberty Hall. There she stood, frail and exhausted, over-awed by her reception. It must have been a wonderful moment for Constance who had endured so much.

When she was sentenced to life in prison there had seemed no point in keeping Surrey House so Constance now found herself homeless. Dr Kathleen Lynn took her to her own home and nursed her back to health. As soon as she was well enough she fulfilled a wish she had had since that final night in the College of Surgeons – she became a Catholic.

THE RISE OF SINN FÉIN

Constance did not have much time to recuperate. Within weeks of her release she was helping Eamon de Valera, now also free, to fight a by-election in East Clare. At Ennis her speeches were so strongly Republican that one evening she was attacked by the relatives of soldiers fighting in World War I. She was protected from the mob by a group of local Sinn Féiners who barred their way as Con fled down a side-street to safety. These were dangerous times but Constance never flinched from doing or saying what she believed no matter what the consequences.

De Valera astounded the country with a landslide victory in the election. The next by-election was also won by the Sinn Féin candidate. The success of the party at the polls roused new fears in Government circles. Passions were running high at these elections and in the hopes of cooling things down the authorities decided to arrest some of the Sinn Féin leaders. One of them, Thomas Ashe, died in prison after being forcibly fed while on hunger strike. Like the executions in 1916 his death only made Sinn Féin more popular.

In October 1917 Sinn Féin held their Ard Fheis. They elected de Valera as their new President, and Griffith as Vice President. Constance and Michael Collins, the young man who had recited Emmet's speech in Con's home, were elected to the party's Executive Council. Constance was also honoured by being made spokeswoman for labour affairs. The party now set out to secure international recognition for Ireland as an independent Irish Republic. As World War I was being fought to safeguard the independence of small nations the Sinn Féin leaders believed that Ireland's right to self-government could no longer be ignored.

The war continued in Europe with huge loss of life on both sides. In April 1918 the British Army was desperate for more troops and Parliament passed a law imposing conscription (compulsory military service) on Ireland. The country was outraged and every organisation, with the exception of the Ulster Unionists, united to oppose it.

Constance, through Cumann na mBan and the Irish Women Workers' Union, led the womens' resistance to conscription. They hung a huge banner from the top floor of Liberty Hall saying 'We serve neither King nor Kaiser.' She organised a flag day and went around addressing anti-conscription meetings. Once again the Government became alarmed and decided to arrest the leaders of Sinn Féin. Between 17 and 18 May 1918, seventy-three people were rounded up to be interned in England. Michael Collins had been tipped off about the arrests by a Sinn Féin spy in the Castle. He warned the leaders but they decided not to resist as the propaganda value of being interned without trial would be enormous.

Con was on her way home from visiting Maud Gonne McBride when she was arrested. Maud Gonne and Kathleen Clarke, Tom Clarke's widow were also arrested, and all three were sent to Holloway Prison in London. For Constance being an internee was much easier than being a convict serving hard labour. She settled down quite happily in Holloway – which was just as well because Maud Gonne and Kathleen Clarke were released before her on grounds of ill health.

The war ended in 1918 while she was still in prison and a general election was immediately called. Sinn Féin decided to contest every seat in Ireland. They promised that if elected they would not take their seats at Westminster but would set up a parliament or dáil in Dublin. Constance Markievicz's name was put forward for St. Patrick's Division in Dublin. She managed to send out an election address from Holloway and her friends canvassed for her in Dublin. Over half the candidates in the election were in jail. When the results were announced on the 28 December 1918, the Home Rule party had won six seats, the Unionists twenty-six and Sinn Féin an astounding seventy-three.

Countess Constance Markievicz was the only woman elected in the whole of the United Kingdom of Great Britain and Ireland as it then was. This gave her the unique distinction of being the first woman ever to be elected to the British Parliament. Because of Sinn Féin policy she never took her seat. On her release from Holloway she visited the House of Commons just to see her name over the coat peg alloted to her in the members' cloakroom.

MINISTER FOR LABOUR

As promised before the election Sinn Féin set up an Irish parliament. When Dáil Eireann met for the first time in the Mansion House in Dublin on the 21 January 1919, Constance and the majority of those elected were still in jail. By the time it met again in April the leaders, including Constance, had been freed. Eamon de Valera was re-elected President, Griffith his deputy, Michael Collins, Minister for Finance and Constance Markievicz was appointed Minister for Labour. Thus she became the first woman cabinet minister in Europe.

At first the Government treated them as a farce but when the shadow government set up their own courts and tried to collect taxes, the Government took action. Just a month after her release from Holloway Constance was arrested for the third time. This time she was charged with making a treasonable speech in which she used Jonathan Swift's famous remark. 'Burn everything British but its coal.' She was sent to Cork prison for four months. By the time she was released in October, Sinn Féin, the Dáil and all nationalist organisations had been declared illegal.

The ban had been declared because guerrilla warfare had broken out between the old Volunteers, now called the Irish Republican Army (I.R.A.), and the Black and Tans. The 'Tans' were a group of ruthless ex-soldiers and ex-convicts brought in from England to back up the armed Irish police force. Their nickname came from their uniform which was a mixture of army khaki and the black and green caps and belts of the Irish police. They were under no proper discipline and took the law into their own hands. They roamed the country in a reign of terror. The war between the Tans and the Republicans escalated with terrible atrocities committed on both sides. Yeats described the horror of the times vividly:

Now days are dragon-ridden, the nightmare
Rides upon sleep; a drunken soldier
Can leave the mother, murdered at her door,
To crawl in her own blood, and go scot-free.

It was against this background that Constance and the other ministers had to work. They were on the run day and night from the police. But Con revelled in this new challenge. She told Eva, 'I don't know whether I am most like the timid hare, the wily fox or a fierce wild animal of the jungle ... Every house is open to me and everyone is ready to help.' She had many lucky escapes thanks to the loyal people of Dublin who gave her sanctuary as she kept one step ahead of the police.

During this time she was nicknamed 'Charlie's Aunt' because she moved about the city wearing an ancient bonnet trimmed with cherries and stooped like an old woman. She was even helped across the road by a policeman one day and as soon as he was out of sight she danced a merry jig.

Despite all the difficulties she continued her work as Minister for Labour and her efficiency inspired her staff. She had a ladder permanently placed at her office window so that she could make a quick get-away. On one occasion Constance, tipped off that the police were on their way, had just enough time to pile important papers into an old trunk and rush off with it in a taxi. At first she could not think what to do with the trunk, then she remembered a friend of hers had a second-hand shop opposite the Black and Tans' headquarters. She couldn't resist a wry smile as she watched her friend place the valuable trunk in the window marked 'For Sale £3'.

Eventually her luck ran out. Driving back from a trip to the Wicklow mountains Con was stopped for having no tail lamp. She was recognised and arrested. Back in Mountjoy she immediately sent word to Eva, who always worried about her, that she was well and cheerful. The fact that she was allowed to work in the garden helped. She loved nature and she always kept crumbs for the birds in her cell.

Yeats, who did not agree with her out-spoken politics, wrote in his poem 'On a Political Prisoner':

She that but little patience knew
From childhood on, had now so much.
A grey gull lost its fear and flew
Down to her cell and there alit
And there endured her fingers' touch
And from her fingers ate its bit.

He understood well how hard it was for Constance to be locked up.

Constance dressed for combat.

In the spring of 1920, Lloyd George passed the Government of Ireland Act through Parliament. This Act set up two parliaments in Ireland instead of just one as proposed in the 1914 Home Rule Act. The northern Parliament was to rule six Ulster counties and the southern Parliament the other twenty-six. The Act was accepted by the Unionists in the north but was rejected by the rest of the country. The following year Stormont, the northern Parliament, was opened.

The guerrilla war continued and grew more vicious as the months passed. On Sunday 21 November the savagery reached its peak. Early that morning a group of eleven Englishmen, believed by the I.R.A. leaders to be an undercover assassination group sent to wipe them out, were shot while still in their beds. That afternoon, as a reprisal for the killings, the Black and Tans surrounded Croke Park during a Gaelic football match and fired into the crowd, killing twelve people and injuring sixty. This terrible day became known as 'Bloody Sunday'.

People in Ireland and England were shocked by these awful events. In England many fair-minded people, including the Archbishop of Canterbury, began to demand peace. In July 1921, after lengthy talks between Lloyd George and de Valera, a truce was finally arranged. With the truce the Irish prisoners were released and Constance was free again.

THE TREATY

The truce was obeyed by both sides. Now all that needed to be done was to acknowledge the end of the war officially by making a peace treaty between the leaders of Ireland and England.

In October 1921, an Irish delegation led by Arthur Griffith and Michael Collins went to London to negotiate the peace terms with the British Prime Minister Lloyd George and his advisers. De Valera, who had earlier arranged the truce, refused to go even though he was now the official Irish Head of State. The Irish delegates were *envoys plenipotentiaries*, that is they had full power to make an agreement and sign it.

The negotiations dragged on day and night for weeks. Finally on the 6 December 1921, the Treaty was signed. The Irish had not been granted the full independent Republic that they sought but they accepted the proposals as a stepping stone to complete independence. The night before they signed Lloyd George had threatened the Irish 'sign now or war will resume'.

News of the Treaty was greeted with relief at home. The Irish were war weary and wanted an end to the terror and bloodshed. The Treaty could only come into effect if accepted by both Parliaments. As soon as the delegates returned to Dublin the Dáil met to debate the terms. De Valera, Constance and others were against accepting the Treaty which excluded the six counties of Ulster and included a clause insisting on an Oath of Allegiance to the Crown (the King of England). During the debate they spoke bitterly of having been betrayed. They wanted a full thirty-two county Republic and nothing less. But many others were in favour. After weeks of rancour, a vote was finally taken and a majority of Dáil deputies voted in favour. The Treaty was then ratified.

Sadly, when it became law de Valera and his followers, including Constance, walked out of the Dáil. They did not return in Con's lifetime. The remaining members formed a new Government with Arthur Griffith as President.

Constance, of course, ceased to be Minister for Labour. De Valera and those who refused to accept the Treaty set up a new Republican party, Cumann na Poblachta, which Con now joined. The new party sent her to America to raise funds for the Irish Republic they still hoped to achieve. In America she was treated as a celebrity. They called her 'Ireland's Joan of Arc' and were surprised by her gentle and fragile appearance. Her tour was a great success. Con loved America and its modern ways and even took up the

American habit of chewing gum.

When the liner docked in England on her return journey, Con stopped for a few days in London to see Maeve who was living there. Maeve was now twenty years of age. They had not met since Con was in Cork jail and her appearance had changed so much that a friend had to point her out to Maeve. The long spells in prison had taken their toll and many noticed how frail and careworn she had become.

CIVIL WAR

While she was away Ireland had become more divided over the Treaty. Shortly after her return Con lost her seat in an election. Then tragically civil war broke out between those who wanted a republic and those who accepted what the Treaty had given them – a Free State. When the fighting started Con joined her fellow Republicans on the roofs of O'Connell Street. She is remembered as being in the thick of the action picking off Free State snipers as she crouched behind a chimney stack. The civil war was fought with as much ferocity as the earlier war with the Black and Tans. But this time it was brother against brother.

The war ended after a year in June 1922 and in August Con won back her seat at the general election which followed. Like the other elected Republicans she refused to take her seat in the Dáil because of the Oath of Allegiance. But outside the Dáil she was as busy as ever. Many Republicans were still in prison. They had been arrested by the Irish Government for their part in the civil war. Constance believed that as the war was over they should all be freed. She spent her time campaigning on their behalf. Wherever a crowd was gathered in the street you could be sure it was 'the Countess holding a meeting for the release of the prisoners'. During one of these meetings she was arrested for causing a breach of the peace and sent to prison yet again.

She was released in time for Christmas 1923 and in the new year was back at her political activities. She presided

*Fighting during the Civil War – now it was brother
against brother.*

at Cumann na mBan meetings, reorganised the Fianna, was associated with St. Ultan's children's hospital, and was a member of the Rathmines Urban District Council. On the Council her main concern was for the poorer sections of society. She fought hard to secure better housing, health and child care for the people she represented.

Out of the blue she had a visit from Casimir. He was on a diplomatic mission to London and came over to Dublin to see Constance. They found that they had little in common after so many years of separation and Casi soon returned to his native Poland.

After Con's arrest in 1916 Surrey House had been searched and ransacked by the army. When they left, the looters moved in and stole what they could. Constance was left with few possessions and from then on she had no permanent home. She stayed with various friends who generously accepted her into their homes.

She still had a small income which gave her financial independence and now at the age of fifty she decided to buy herself a car. It proved to be a great buy and had many uses. During a coal strike in Dublin in 1926 Con drove the car out to the bogs time and time again to bring back turf for the poor of her constituency. She would pack the car with the much needed fuel and, on her return, haul the heavy bags on her back up the rickety tenement stairs to the old and needy.

Her charity among the poor of Dublin was legendary. If anyone was in want and Con had money she just gave it away. She even sold a lovely ring her mother left her, one of her few valuable possessions, to save a family from eviction. It was these spontaneous acts of kindness that made 'the Countess' a much loved figure among Dublin's poor.

FINAL CAMPAIGN

Since her meeting with Maeve in London, Con had grown closer to her daughter. Now, on her way to and from Sligo,

Maeve always called to stay with her mother and Constance looked forward to these visits. Lady Gore-Booth, who was still alive, saw Con from time to time when she visited Dublin but there is no doubt that she and the rest of the family found it, as Constance herself said, 'very embarrassing to have a relation that gets into jail and fights in revolutions that you are not in sympathy with'.

This is probably the reason why she did not go to England when her beloved sister Eva died. Word of Eva's death reached Con in June 1926 while she was fighting an election campaign as a member of de Valera's new Fianna Fáil party. Con told a friend that she did not attend the funeral because she could not 'face the family'. News of Eva's death left her in a state of shock. They had been lifelong friends and Eva in her gentle way was a great support to Con throughout her life. They were as close and loving to one another as two sisters can be. While Con was recovering from the loss of Eva her mother died.

Many of her friends thought she looked ill during this period and wanted her to see a doctor but she refused point blank, saying she had no time as there was an election to be fought. She threw all her energy into electioneering so as to forget her sadness. One day, on her way to an election meeting, she was trying to start the car when the starting handle slipped and broke her arm. Undeterred she told the doctor who was setting it, 'it's lucky it's only my arm. I can still talk!' and rushed off to her meeting. Constance was re-elected. Fianna Fáil won forty-four seats. De Valera and the newly elected members of his party, including Con with her arm in a sling, tried to enter the Dáil without taking the Oath of Allegiance but the doors were locked against them. They were to return and take their seats but sadly this time it would be without Constance.

At the end of June she became seriously ill and was sent to Sir Patrick Dun's Hospital. She insisted on being in a public ward with her fellow Dubliners. She was operated on for appendicitis and seemed to be recovering when complications set in. She became gravely ill. Maeve was with her at her bedside. Casimir and her much loved stepson, Stasko, came from Poland after hearing an emergency message on the radio. When they arrived with a huge box of roses Constance perked up enough to tell them, 'This is the happiest day of my life.' Esther Roper came over from London and found the hospital besieged with well wishers. In the street outside her ward faithful Dubliners prayed that she would get better. There was only one question on all their lips 'How is the Countess?' They waited anxiously and wept openly when, on the 15 July 1927, they heard she had died. She died in the public ward surrounded by her family, friends and the poor of Dublin.

Her body lay in state in the Pillar Room of the Rotunda for two days. Her Fianna boys acted as guard of honour as 100,000 people filed past the coffin. Thousands lined the streets of Dublin to say farewell. One old woman who had promised to bring three fresh eggs to the hospital for Constance, left them in the coffin to fulfill her promise. Constance was buried in Glasnevin Cemetery in the Republican plot with her old comrades. This had been her wish. De Valera said at her graveside: 'Madame Markievicz is gone from us, Madame, the friend of the toiler, the lover of the poor. Ease and station she put aside and took the hard way of service with the weak and downtrodden. Sacrifice, misunderstanding and scorn lay on the road she adopted, but she trod it unflinchingly ... It is sadly we take our leave but we pray high heaven that all she longed for may one day be achieved.'

Countess Constance Markievicz was one of Ireland's most outstanding women and probably one of the most remarkable women of the twentieth century. This aristocratic lady's unselfish service to Ireland should not be forgotten. She strove for political and social justice for the Irish nation and its people against tremendous odds. She was indeed the 'Rebel Countess'.

BIBLIOGRAPHY

Bromage Mary, *De Valera and the March of a Nation* (London 1956)

Caulfield Max, *The Easter Rebellion* (London 1964)

Fingall Elizabeth Countess of, *Seventy Years Young* (London 1937)

Haverty Anne, *Constance Markievicz* (London 1988)

Jones Francis P., *History of Sinn Féin Movement and the Irish Rebellion of 1916* (New York 1919)

Lewis Gifford, *Eva Gore-Booth and Esther Roper* (London 1988)

Marreco Ann, *The Rebel Countess* (Philadelphia 1967)

O Faoláin Seán, *Constance Markievicz* (London 1938)

Roper Esther (ed), *Prison Letters of Countess Markievicz* (London 1934)

Ryan Desmond, *The Rising* (Dublin 1949)

Yeats W.B., *Collected Poems* (London 1982)

Younger Carlton, *Ireland's Civil War* (London 1968)

The Royal Commission of the Irish Rebellion (London 1916)

The authors and publishers wish to thank the following for permission to reprint the following illustrations and photographs: Bord Failte page 6; Lafayette Studios page 26; The National Library pages 12, 39 and 59; Sligo Museum, Kilgannon Collection page 21; University College Dublin Archive page 68.

PLACES TO GO AND THINGS TO SEE

DUBLIN

Surrey House, Rathmines – nicknamed 'Scurry House',
Constance and Casimir moved here in 1912
College of Surgeons, St. Stephen's Green – Constance
held this building against attack during the 1916 Rising
St. Stephen's Green Park – statue of Constance
Kilmainham Jail – Constance was imprisoned here
Liberty Hall – this building replaced the old Liberty Hall
General Post Office – headquarters of the rebels during
the 1916 Rising
National Museum – artifacts from the Rising
Tom Clarke's shop, Parnell Street – meeting place for na-
tionalists
Glasnevin Cemetery – leaders of the Rising buried here
Abbey Theatre – some of Casimir's plays were staged
here

CO. SLIGO

Lissadell – Constance's family home is now open to the
public
Sligo Museum – artifacts of Constance's life
Drumcliff – schoolhouse where Constance held public
meeting

CO. LAOIS

The Veteran Car Museum, Portlaoise – car that belonged
to Constance

YEAR	CONSTANCE MARKIEVICZ	IRELAND	WORLD
1868	Constance, born 4 February		British Empire leading world power Music: Verdi, Wagner, Strauss Art: Renoir, Monet, Cezanne, Degas
1870		Gladstone's first Land Act	Dickens writes his last book
1871			Bismarck becomes Chancellor of newly united Germany
1875		Parnell elected MP	
1876			Telephone invented.
1879		Land League formed by Davitt and Parnell	Edison invents electric light
1881		Gladstone's second Land Act	
1882	Joins the Sligo Hunt, aged 14		First *Sherlock Holmes* book published
1885			Twain's *Huckleberry Finn* published
1886		Defeat of Home Rule	Queen Victoria's Golden Jubilee
1887	Presented at Court to Queen Victoria	First All-Ireland Final played	
1888			Van Gogh 'Sunflowers'
1891		Death of Parnell	
1893	Constance at the Slade Art School, London	Second Home Rule Bill defeated Gaelic League founded	

1896	Forms Suffragette group in Sligo		First modern Olympic Games in Athens
1897	Goes to study art in Paris		
1899	Engaged to Count Markievicz		Boer War breaks out in South Africa
1900	Sir Henry Gore-Booth dies, Constance marries in London		
1901	Daughter Maeve born at Lissadell		
1903	Returns to live in Dublin	Wyndham Land Act passed	Suffragette movement begins in Britain
1905		Sinn Féin founded	Einstein's Theory of Relativity published
1906			First radio programme of voice and music broadcast. Picasso painting
1907	Finds old nationalist newspapers in cottage		
1908	Attends her first Sinn Féin meeting	National University set up	Grahame publishes *Wind in the Willows*
1909	Sets up Fianna Eireann with Bulmer Hobson	Larkin founds the ITGWU	University College Dublin and Queen's University Belfast open
1912	Helps set up food kitchens in city-centre schools		Widespread labour unrest in Britain leads to large-scale strikes, *Titanic* sinks,
1913	Sets up food kitchen in Liberty Hall	Lock Out strike in Dublin. Irish Volunteers founded	
1914		Home Rule Bill passed	Outbreak of World War I
1915	Honoured by ITGWU	O'Donovan-Rossa funeral	

1916	Arrested and sentenced to death, reprieved and sent to Aylesbury Jail	Easter Rising	Battle of Somme, more than a million casualties
1917	Released from Aylesbury Jail, elected to Executive Council of Sinn Féin	Sinn Féin wins by-election	Russian Revolution, Tsar abdicates, Lenin becomes leader
1918	Arrested and sent to Holloway Prison, wins seat in election	Conscription crisis Landslide victories for Sinn Féin in elections	End World War I Women over 30 get vote in Britain
1919	Appointed Minister for Labour Arrested and sent to Cork Jail	Dáil Eireann meets	
1920	Arrested again and sent to Mountjoy Prison	Black and Tans in Ireland Government of Ireland Act	Gandhi leading opposition to British rule in India
1921		Truce, Northern Ireland Parliament opens, Treaty talks	
1922	Fights in Civil War	Civil War Michael Collins killed Civil War ends	Mussolini comes to power in Italy T.S. Eliot 'The Wasteland' James Joyce Ulysses
1923	Arrested		
1924			First Labour Government in Britain
1926	Re-elected Eva dies	First Irish radio station School attendance made compulsory	
1927	Constance dies		